DISC

PENGUINS

Rourke Enterprises, Inc.
Vero Beach, Florida 32964

PHOTO CREDITS

© M. P. Kahl/DRK Photo: Cover, title page,
Pages 4, 7, 12-13, 15, 18;
© Sue Matthews/DRK Photo: Page 8;
© Stanley Breeden/DRK Photo: Page 10;
© Annie Griffiths/DRK Photo: Page 17;
© Lynn M. Stone: Page 21

Library of Congress Cataloging-in-Publication Data

Stone, Lynn M.
    Penguins / by Lynn M. Stone

    p. cm. — (Bird discovery library)
    Includes index.
    Summary: Describes the appearance, habits, habitat, daily life,
infancy, and enemies of the bird that travels on land and in the
water but not in the air.
    ISBN 0-86592-325-6
    1. Penguins—Juvenile literature. [1. Penguins.] I. Title.
II. Series: Stone, Lynn M. Bird discovery library.
QL696.S473S75 1989   88-31606
598.4'41 - dc19   CIP
                                                    AC

TABLE OF CONTENTS

PENGUINS

Penguins look like little men in white shirts and black suits. They stand upright on short legs and webbed feet. Their wings hang loosely like arms.

Penguins are the world's only group of **flightless** diving birds. Their wings are useless for flight. Penguins do all their traveling by land or by sea.

There are 18 different kinds, or **species,** of penguins on earth. All live in the southern half of the world. They rest and nest on shores, but they hunt in cool or cold ocean water.

Puffins and auks look and act much like penguins, but these birds live in northern oceans and they fly.

Adelie Penguin
(Pygoscelis adeliae)

WHERE THEY LIVE

Penguins live in the waters of Ecuador, Peru, Chile, Argentina, South Africa, New Zealand, Australia, the Falkland Islands, and Antarctica. Their homes on the seashore may be green meadows, rocky beaches, woods, or the ice of Antarctica. Antarctica is the coldest, windiest place on earth.

Penguins usually come ashore on islands. They avoid the four-footed **predators** which live on the mainland. Predators are larger, stronger animals that might kill them.

The penguin family has adjusted to extremes of weather. The Galapagos penguin *(Spheniscus mendiculus)* lives in Ecuador, South America. Temperatures there rise to 104°F. Temperatures in the Antarctica home of the emperor *(Aptenodytes fosteri)* and Adelie *(Pygoscelis adeliae)* penguins dip to −70°F.

Adelie Penguins

HOW THEY LOOK

Penguins generally have black backs and light bellies. A few species have crests or brightly colored ear patches.

Early penguin viewers wondered whether penguins were birds or fish. Penguins have long, torpedo-shaped bodies, and they look silky smooth, like fish, when they swim. Ashore they are awkward and slow.

The largest penguins are the emperors, which stand up to four feet and weigh up to 90 pounds. The similar king penguins *(Aptenodytes patagonica)* stand up to three feet.

The smallest penguins are the little blues *(Eudyptula minor)* of Australia and New Zealand. They weigh about three pounds.

King Penguins
(Aptenodytes patagonica),
Colony at S. Georgia Island

Eye

Beak

Flipper (Wing)

Webbed Foot

THE PENGUIN'S FLIPPERS

The penguin's wings are really flippers. They are flat and strong, similar to a seal's flippers. Seal flippers, however, are covered with skin. Penguin flippers are covered by tiny, stiff feathers.

Flippers power the penguin underwater. Penguins can not fly in the air, but they can "fly" underwater at about five miles per hour.

The first penguin-like birds millions of years ago could fly. But the ability to swim well became more important to penguins than flying. Their food was in the sea, and they didn't have many animal enemies on land. Slowly the wings, which they didn't really need, became better suited for swimming than for flying.

Little Blue Penguin
(Fairy Penguin)
(Eudyptula minor)

Adelie Penguins

THE PENGUIN'S DAY

Penguin activities vary according to the season and the species of penguin. Sooner or later, all penguins spend much of their time at sea. There they are most at home. Penguins depend on the sea for food, and sometimes they remain at sea for many days.

When penguins splash ashore, they live together in large groups, or **colonies.** Each species stays with its own kind.

Penguins in the colonies often jab at each other with sharp beaks and "argue" back and forth. Penguin colonies are loud, crowded, and smelly.

PENGUIN NESTS

Most penguins, especially those near and in Antarctica, nest in large colonies. Some colonies contain over one million penguins. One known colony of Adelie penguins has five million. One colony of chinstrap penguins *(Pygoscelis antarctica)* has over ten million birds!

Penguins generally lay two eggs, although the big emperors and kings lay just one.

Some penguins nest in burrows. Others lay eggs between rocks, among tree roots, or in caves. Penguin nests are usually lined with sticks or pebbles.

The emperors and kings do not have nests of any kind. The males of both species **incubate** their one egg on the top of their feet. A flap of skin droops over the egg and keeps it warm against the penguin's feet for several weeks.

Jackass Penguin Nest and Egg

BABY PENGUINS

Baby king penguins are nearly naked when they hatch. Young emperor penguins and most other species are covered by warm, fluffy feathers known as **down.**

Baby penguins grow up on a diet of fish and other sea creatures. They don't hunt for themselves, however. Their parents feed them. The adults force food up from their own stomachs to feed the babies.

As they grow, penguins build up a layer of fat or **blubber.** The blubber helps them keep warm.

Penguins begin hunting for themselves after their adult feathers replace the down.

Gentoo Penguin with Young

PREDATORS AND PREY

Penguins are **predators.** They feed upon other animals—fish, squid, and a shrimp-like animal called **krill.**
Penguins dive and use their beaks to catch their **prey,** the animals that they eat. Penguins swim to the surface every two or three minutes for air. Penguins usually dive 50 or 60 feet deep, but emperor penguins have dived to 875 feet!

Penguins share the southern seas with other animals. Penguins are prey for some of these animals, especially the leopard seal. Adult penguins are also eaten by sharks. Penguin eggs and babies are eaten by several birds, such as the **skua.**

Rockhopper Penguin
(Eudyptes crestatus) swimming

PENGUINS AND PEOPLE

In the 1700's and 1800's penguins were killed by the thousands. Explorers and whale boat crews ate them and used the skins of at least one species, the king penguin, for clothing. Penguin blubber was boiled into oil for fuel.

There is no longer any need to kill penguins. Everywhere they live, they are protected by laws. Today, millions of penguins live on and around the islands of the southern oceans.

Most penguin species are doing well. But people are moving more of their activities toward Antarctica. The future safety of the birds in the "black suits" will depend on our protecting their homes.

GLOSSARY

Blubber (BLUH ber)—a protective layer of fat on animals in cold climates

Colonies (KAHL uh neez)—a group of nesting animals of the same kind

Down (DOWN)—soft, tiny feathers

Flightless (FLITE less)—a bird without the ability to fly, such as ostriches and penguins

Incubate (INK u bate)—to keep eggs warm until they hatch

Krill (KRILL)—various, small shrimp-like animals of the cold seas

Predator (PRED a tor)—an animal which kills another for food

Prey (PRAY)—an animal which is hunted for food by another animal

Skua (SKYOU ah)—large, gull-like bird

Species (SPEE sheez)—within a group of closely-related animals, such as penguins, one certain kind or type

INDEX